She Healed In Love

BETH

BookLeaf
Publishing

She Healed In Love © 2023 BETH

All rights reserved.

No part of this publication may be reproduced, stored in a retrieval system, or transmitted, in any form or by any means, electronic, mechanical, photocopying, recording, or otherwise, without the prior written permission of the presenters.

BETH asserts the moral right to be identified as the author of this work.

Presentation by *BookLeaf Publishing*

Web: www.bookleafpub.com

E-mail: info@bookleafpub.com

ISBN: 9789357211741

First edition 2023

DEDICATION

To the souls who showed me the type of love that heals you - these are your love letters. I would not be here without you.

ACKNOWLEDGEMENT

To the people who embraced me in the expression of my vulnerability, I am universally grateful for your kindness and absolute love. Through you, I found strength and the courage to pour inward - I hope to one day spread that light unto others as you did to me.

PREFACE

With new seasons of life come the pains of growing anew and discovering old truths you never saw (or dared) to realise. If you're lucky, you find people who guide you through the darkness. If you're luckier, you find yourself to hold onto through it all.

This book is an ode to the beauties in my life. To the things and the people who painted colour in my season. To the soul friends who become lovers because of how they love you so, and the memories they create that gift the hope of possibility.

May those moments never cease and those people be cherished endlessly.

One.

Write, my darling.
Pour your soul into ink.

Let tear-stained parchment speak the words you
never dare.

Spend hours and pages harnessing the human song
knowing words are never fit to paint the colours of
your ether.

Let the pen fly,
across countless lines of paper.

Like a wildfire amongst grasslands,
let it run and forge its path.

Watch the letters come to be
and feel the glitter in each phrase.

It is the glimmer of your soul. The purest form of your
expression.

Two.

I pray you find those who hold starlight in their eyes.

The people who glow from the sunlight in their souls.

And when you meet them, my dear, may you cry to
the winds,

"So these are the ones who make life so remarkable."

Three.

Human, yet too angelic.
She exists somewhere in between.

Indescribable through language,
she is something else entirely.

To be painted. To be mused.
Her mere existence inspires art.

She is pure grace, embodied.
The wonder of life, eternal.

Four.

I looked into her eyes and saw myself, but not.
Two hearts - separate - yet moulded by twin palms.

Each curve, every imprint, and intended scar.
We had lived the same stories and shared the same
scores.

Like siblings returning home
from mirrored journeys in different lands.

There was a comfort - an understanding - of whom
we'd been and would become.

A wave of love in a most intimate form,
of connection at the soul through language beyond
words.

I smiled - as did she - and something brewed within.

Perhaps moments such as these are how magic is
born.

Five.

Keep close the people who can be with you and not crowd you. The ones whose hearts strengthen the rhythm of your own. To have souls who see you and wish others to do so, without agenda nor malice, is a gift rarely received. If you find them, savour them. Let gratitude flood your heart. For the goodness of pure intention is worth a lifetime of the sublime.

Six.

To her eyes that sparkle
and her smile which glows.

To her hugs that tickle your soul into joy.

In melody, her voice
will soothe and sing so sweetly.

Close your eyes.
Dance.
She will paint you into expression.

Like the rivers of water shall her currents of love flow.

May you be nourished by her tranquillity
and be revived to live life brightly.

Seven.

To write without expectation - what a marvellous thing.

As the words pour forth while the pen grips your heart.

Let emotions tell their tale. Let them divulge all they yearn.

And may you sit back in awe at the masterpieces you create.

Eight.

Eyes. Sea-green.
Like the ocean, mirrored. Deep and spiralled into a
quiet world of wonder.

In pools of sage with flecks of deep ochre,
there lies a spirit in those waters, a dancer of all
dances.

Her soul echoes the wind as her heartbeat calls her
home.
Ever moving - never quite still - she drifts with the tide.

She was called from fairy and her flow echoes such.
There's a quietness to her presence. Find stillness to
hear it sing.

Delicately before us in her grace may you unfold,
and she will hold, in her Dharma, abundant space for
your soul.

Nine.

Perhaps angels do exist.
She certainly does.

Ten.

Find your music and press play.

Let the notes sing loud as they echo into the void.

Through paint, through words, through language,
through love.

Let it touch every soul and ignite the magic within.

Eleven

She will hold you in her arms and bathe you in sunlight.

Inhale her warmth,
let it fill your lungs entirely.

What some call Spring I simply call, Her.

Just as sweet
and ever so magical.

Twelve.

I intend to marvel at Earth's artistry before me. To admonish bitter hate and relinquish vices to the skies. With every shell and layer I shall bathe and wash away, let me be cleansed and reborn into new light and new love.

Thirteen.

She is honey, but sweeter.
Like honey warmed by the sun.
One droplet of her soul will have you nourished from
head to toe.

Bubbly and fizzy,
her nature sings out joy.

She will hold you in her heart
and refuse to let you go.

Fourteen.

You were born from stardust, my child, and to stardust shall you one day return. But take with care and mind with heart the sparkle that can shine throughout. As the atoms within you once danced amongst the moons, so too will you dance through this version of life. And like the suns and galaxies into which you gaze above, so too are you surrounded by the purest forms of magic.

Fifteen.

She embodied an old soul with that youthful glow.
With the kind of eyes that twinkle for the vigour of life's
mysteries.

Her laugh was like daisies as they bloom with Spring
dawn. She is both the dolphin beneath the waters and
the dragonfly soaring the skies.

Surrendering to Spirit does she dance her way through
life. Find yourself pulled close by some magnetic, holy
force.

Across centuries and worlds she seems to know the
Way. Painting brushstrokes and colours in that deeper
shade of gold.

She reminds you of the splendour that this life is here
to gift you, and may she awaken you renewed to relish
all that comes to be.

Sixteen.

On my knees may I cry and weep tears to the Earth.
And may the Mother grow wildflowers to bloom this
heartache into hope.

Seventeen.

I gazed my chin to the sky and felt the rain kiss my cheek.

In the arms of the Mother I was home. I was safe.

Beyond the bruising winds and the voices that thunder,

I found a haven of serenity and met myself inside it.

Eighteen.

She was sunlight in a bottle.
The warmest glow of a Summer's day.

Enwrapping you in love,
she could soften every scar.

Full of energy, of life, of everything good and whole,
she reminds you of the splendour that this world may
yet bestow.

Palms open, heart full, breathe into the beauty.
In the presence of her being let her nature kiss you
sweetly.

Behind the trail of her footsteps lie the dustings of
pixies,
a playful dance do those imprints mark for you to
follow.

So smile, leap forward, twirl into the movement.
And may you one day discover it was *yourself* leading
the way.

www.ingramcontent.com/pod-product-compliance
Lightning Source LLC
La Vergne TN
LVHW050302200726

843509LV00015B/3124